30°E 60° 90° 120° 150°

Arctic Ocean

A S I A

E U R O P E

GREECE

AFRICA

Pacific

Ocean

Indian

Ocean

AUSTRALIA

ANTARCTICA

Greece

Jen Green

Greg Anderson and Kostas Vlassopoulos, Consultants

NATIONAL GEOGRAPHIC

WASHINGTON, D.C.

Contents

E ven after more than 2,000 years, the ancient culture of Greece still has a considerable impact on the modern world. Greek words like democracy, philosophy, history, theater, and physics are still used to describe some of the most fundamental aspects of our society. And the problems that ancient Greek artists and thinkers wrestled with are highly relevant to us today. For example, Greek tragedies and other dramas allow us to explore human suffering and help us find our place in the modern world. In addition, we are still dealing with political issues that were first debated in ancient Athens, many centuries ago.

However, modern Greece is equally fascinating because it remains a complex crossroad of civilizations. In addition to being a land with a long heritage, Greece is now a member of the European Union and has been heavily influenced by Western Europe in the last two centuries. At the same time, its music, dances, food, and customs link Greece to the Turkish and Arabic world of the eastern Mediterranean. What is more, its Orthodox religion creates strong bonds with the Slavic world to the north. Greeks have settled in most countries of the world—the third biggest Greek city is actually in Australia!

This variability and diversity also characterizes the land, as this book ably demonstrates. Many people who only visit Greece in the summer go away with an image of a hot and dry land. But the landscape keeps changing in color the whole year around. It is hard to imagine that the flower-covered countryside of spring will become yellowed and dry in just a few months time.

The hundreds of islands that dot the Aegean and the other seas

around Greece create an environment unique to Europe. Despite their many similarities, every Greek island has its particular landscape, customs, history, and even dialect, thus creating innumerable small worlds, all worth exploring. Within a single island one can find many things. For example, the largest Greek island, Crete, has alpine vegetation and snow-covered mountains in the west and desert-like conditions in the east.

With its age-old traditions and spectacular landscapes, Greece has many things to offer the world. I hope you will see for yourself one day.

▲ A ferry picks up cars and passengers from a small island town. Ferries criss-cross Greek waters every day, connecting the country's many islands with the mainland—and carrying tourists enjoying an "island-hopping" vacation.

Kostas Vlassopoulos

Kostas Vlassopoulos
University of Nottingham,
United Kingdom

Rugged Beauty

GREECE IS PROBABLY BEST known for its islands. Visitors from all over Europe and other parts of the world spend their vacations on one of about 50 islands in the Aegean Sea. They leave with memories of blue seas, sandy beaches, and whitewashed villages. But there is a lot more to Greece. The country's mainland has rugged mountains, dense forests, and lakes. It also has many remarkable ancient sites that are evidence of the country's history as the birthplace of Western culture. Greece holds many surprises. With its long history, who would guess that the area has been a single state for less than 200 years? Did you know that there are two different versions of the Greek language, or that half of all Greeks live abroad?

◀ A centuries-old village sits on the cliffs of Thíra (Santorini), an island in the Aegean Sea. This island belongs to the Cyclades, one of five main groups of Greek islands.

WHAT'S THE WEATHER LIKE?

Greece has a climate typical of southern Europe, with hot, dry summers and mild, wet winters. However, conditions vary in different regions, depending on height above sea level and closeness to the sea. Mountains have cooler temperatures than lowland regions, and it often snows in winter. Sea breezes keep coasts and islands cool in summer and warm in winter. Northern Greece has a more varied climate, with cold winters and hot, sticky summers. The north and west are generally wetter than the south and east. The map opposite shows the physical features of Greece. Labels on this map and on similar maps throughout this book identify many of the places pictured in each chapter.

Fast Facts

OFFICIAL NAME: Hellenic Republic

FORM OF GOVERNMENT: Parliamentary republic

CAPITAL: Athens

POPULATION: 10,722,816

OFFICIAL LANGUAGE: Greek

CURRENCY: Euro

AREA: 50,942 square miles (131,940 square km)

BORDERING NATIONS: Albania, Former Yugoslavic Republic of Macedonia, Bulgaria, Turkey

HIGHEST POINT: Mount Olympus: 9,570 feet (2,917 m)

LOWEST POINT: Sea level

MAJOR MOUNTAIN RANGES: Pindus, Rhodope, Mount Athos, Óros Taígetus

LONGEST RIVER: Aliákmonas, 200 miles (320 km)

COASTLINE: 9,320 miles (15,000 km)

Average Temperature & Rainfall

Average High/Low Temperatures; Yearly Rainfall

ATHENS (CENTER): 71° F (22° C) / 57° F (14° C); 15 inches (37 cm)

THESSALONIKI (NORTH): 68° F (20° C) / 49° F (9° C); 18 inches (46 cm)

IRÁKLIO (SOUTH): 71° F (22° C) / 59° F (15° C); 19 inches (49 cm)

Ionian Sea

Aegean Sea

Mediterranean Sea

0 mi 100

0 km 100

MAP KEY

Mild

Mediterranean

GREECE

Europe

Africa

Atlantic Ocean

TURKEY

BULGARIA

MACEDONIA

ALBANIA

Rhodope

Nestos

Xánthi

Strimónas

Thessaloníki (Salonica)

Axiós

Aliákmon

Mount Olympus (Highest point in Greece) 9,570 ft 2,917 m

+ Mount Athos

Pindus Mountains

Pindós

Lárissa

Vólos

Northern Sporades

Lésvos

Évia (Euboea)

Híos

Izmir (Smyrna)

TURKEY

Aegean Sea

Athens

Pireás

Kallithéa

Corinth Canal

Corinth

Peloponnesus

Oros Taígetos

Kalamáta

Pátra

Kérkira (Corfu)

Kefalonia

Ionian Sea

Cyclades

Thíra (Santorini)

Dodecanese

Ródos (Rhodes)

Sea of Crete

Iráklio

Crete

Mediterranean Sea

Évros

STEEP, ROCKY PEAKS, page 10 AND HORSES ON GREEN HILLS, page 12

BARREN MOUNTAIN TOP, page 11

STATUES SUPPORTING BUILDING, page 1 AND FORESTED HILL SURROUNDED BY CITY, page 13

CANAL CUTS THROUGH ROCK, page 10.

CLIFFTOP VILLAGE, pages 2, 6-7 AND SHIPS IN ROCKY BAY, page 13

MAP KEY

⊛ National capital

● Selected city

+ Elevation

miles 0   100

km 0   100

▲ The Meteora are a group of rock pinnacles. *Meteora* means "rocks in the air." In medieval times, monks built homes near the peaks for a peaceful place to live.

Ragged Coastline

Greece is the southernmost country in Europe. Located at the tip of the Balkan Peninsula, it is slightly smaller than the U.S. state of Alabama. Greece has a long, jagged coastline with many inlets that create slender peninsulas jutting into the sea. The country is divided

A COUNTRY DIVIDED

The southern region of Greece is a peninsula called the Peloponnese. It is connected to the mainland by a strip of land just 4 miles (6 km) wide, called the Isthmus of Corinth. In ancient times, sailors used to drag their cargo and sometimes whole ships across the Isthmus to avoid the long voyage around the Peloponnese. In 1893 a ship canal was cut through the Isthmus, linking the Gulf of Corinth to the Aegean Sea. The Corinth Canal (right) is just 75 feet (23 m) wide, so the largest ships cannot use it. However, visitors can stand on one of several bridges to watch cruise ships and freighters pass underneath.

Mount Olympus is Greece's highest peak, 9,570 ft (2,917 m) above sea level. It belongs to the Olympic Range, which is just 12 miles (17 km) long and rises steeply from the sea. Olympus (right) is no ordinary mountain: The ancient Greeks believed it was the home of the gods. According to legend it was the site of a great battle between the gods, led by Zeus, and a race of giants called the Titans. The gods were victorious. The ancient poet Homer described Olympus as a peaceful place above the clouds, with pure air. Its sheer face was first climbed in 1913. In 1937, Mt. Olympus became Greece's first national park.

into three geographical regions: the mainland, the islands, and the Peloponnese, the peninsula just south of the mainland.

Mainland Mountains

Three-quarters of mainland Greece is mountainous. The Pindus range forms a rocky spine that runs north to south. Rising to over 8,530 feet (2,600 m), the Pindus has spectacular limestone landscapes, including the Vikos Gorge. This is one of the world's deepest gorges, plunging 3,600 feet (1,100 m). In the east the Olympic Mountains rise to Greece's highest point, Mount Olympus. The Pindus and Olympic ranges extend into the Peloponnese. They also plunge beneath the sea, where their peaks form several strings of islands.

Crowded Lowlands

Greece's lowlands are mostly narrow strips along the coast. There are also fertile plains inland in Thessaly in central Greece and in Macedonia and Thrace in the north. The lowlands are home to most of the country's population. Two-thirds of Greece's population lives in just eight cities. Athens, the capital, is by far the largest.

▲ Horses graze on the slopes above the plain of Thessaly in central Greece.

Island Groups

Greece has the longest coastline in Europe. Greeks have always looked to the sea for fishing and trading, and they boast one of the largest shipping fleets in the world. Western Greece is bordered by the Ionian Sea; the Mediterranean Sea is to the south, and the Aegean is to the east. There are 3,000 Greek islands, of which only about 100 are inhabited.

The islands are divided into five groups. The Ionian Islands in the west include Kérkira (Corfu) and Kefalonia. The Sporades include Évia (Euboea) and lie east of the mainland, while the North Aegean and Dodecanese Islands hug the Turkish coast. The Cyclades lie in the center, with Crete, Greece's largest island, to the south.

Natural Dangers

Greece lies on a fault line between two of the huge tectonic plates that make up the surface of the Earth.

THE END OF ATLANTIS?

Thíra (Santorini) is a volcanic island in the Aegean Sea. About 3,000 years ago, it was part of the Minoan civilization based in Crete to the south. However, in 1600 B.C., a violent volcanic eruption blew the island apart, creating a huge bay. Seawater poured in, which sent tsunamis rippling across the ocean. Minoan cities on Crete were swamped. Many archaeologists believe the Minoan Empire never recovered. Some people believe the catastrophe gave rise to the legend of Atlantis—the story of an island empire that sank beneath the waves in a night and a day.

▲ Boats dock at Nea Kenami, an island that is surrounded by Thíra and located in the middle of the volcanic bay. It formed only about 400 years ago.

The country is regularly rocked by earthquakes as the plates rub up against each other. In 1999, Athens was hit by a quake that killed 139 people and destroyed almost 3,000 homes.

Geological activity also causes volcanic eruptions. Several Greek islands are really the tips of dormant volcanoes rising from the ocean floor.

▼ Athens is surrounded by mountains on nearly all sides. It also has a steep hill at its center called Mount Lycabettus. A small railroad carries sightseers to the top.

Ancient Groves

FORESTS OF TALL fir trees still cover remote hills in Greece, but 5,000 years ago dense forests covered much of the country. Over the long history of human habitation, Greeks have cut down trees for fuel and lumber and cleared forests to create farms. The remaining forests are mostly in mountains, such as the Pindus and Rhodope ranges.

Located in the southeastern corner of Europe and close to North Africa and Asia, Greece has a rich diversity of plant and animal life drawn from all three regions. Greece has broad-leaved woodlands of beech, oak, and chestnut, similar to the forests of central Europe—but the mountains have conifer forests that would not look out of place in Scandinavia! In the south, Greece has many olive trees, a species that came originally from West Asia.

◀ **A church on the island of Crete is surrounded by ancient olive groves.**

VARIED HABITATS

As well as woodlands and forests, there are alpine meadows high on mountains, grassy plains, and dry, stony areas. The map below shows the main ecoregions—what grows where—in Greece. On coasts, cliffs and sandy coves provide nesting sites for birds and turtles. Wetland habitats, such as salt marshes and freshwater swamps, have been altered by the construction of dams to provide water for farming. Two of the most important remaining wetlands are the Evros Delta and the Mesolongi Lagoons. They are now protected by law. Greece has ten national parks and many more refuges and preserves that protect natural and historical landmarks.

Species at Risk

The main threats to Greece's wildlife come from the destruction of their habitat. Forests have been replaced with fields and pasture. Wetlands, such as coastal marshes, have been drained to provide land for hotels.

Centuries of hunting have made large mammals, such as wolves, brown bears, and boar scarce. Two of Europe's most endangered sea creatures are found in Greek waters: loggerhead turtles and monk seals. Loggerheads are rare because their breeding beaches have been taken over by tourists. Bright lights and noise confuse nesting females and newly hatched young. For centuries the monk seal has been killed by fishers who believe it steals their catch and damages nets. Only a few hundred remain. Luckily, both these species are now protected by marine parks.

Species at risk include:

> Brown bear
> Cretan goat
> European otter
> Hermann's tortoise

> Loggerhead turtle
> Mediterranean monk seal
> Wolf

▼ A baby loggerhead turtle heads down a beach toward the sea after hatching out of its egg.

MAP KEY

Primary Vegetation Zones/Ecosystems

Mediterranean forest, woodlands & scrub

Temperate broadleaf and mixed forest

Protected Lands

Selected national parks

miles

km

BULGARIA

TURKEY

ALBANIA

MACEDONIA

Ionian Sea

Aegean Sea

Mediterranean Sea

Sea of Crete

Rhodope

Évros

Néstos

Strimónas

Axiós

Aliákmonas

Thessaloníki (Salonica)

Olympus N.P.

Pindos N.P.

Pindós

Lárissa

Vólos

Vikos-Aóos N.P.

Prespes N.P.

Kérkira (Corfu)

Pindus Mountains

Mt. Oeta N.P.

Parnassos N.P.

Parnassós

Pátra

Kefalonia

Aínos N.P.

Mesolongi Lagoons

Parnitha N.P.

Piréas

Athens

Sounion N.P.

Peloponnesus

Oros Taígetos

Northern Sporades

Évia (Euboea)

Híos

Lésvos

Dodecanese

Ródos (Rhodes)

Cyclades

Thíra (Santorini)

Iráklio

Crete

Samariá N.P.

BIRD WITH FISH, page 19

FLOWERS AMONG RUINS, page 19

SEABED, page 21

CHURCH IN OLIVE GROVES, pages 2, 14–15 AND **WILD GOAT,** page 18 AND **WHITE TREE TRUNKS ON VILLAGE STREET,** page 21

BABY TURTLE CRAWLS TO THE SEA, page 16

Farmland and Olive Groves

Only about a quarter of Greece is suitable for growing crops. Most other areas are too barren for fields. Instead, they are used as pastures for sheep and goats. Tall, waving cypress trees and groves of olive trees are found all over Greece. Olives have been cultivated in the country for almost 6,000 years, to be eaten as a snack or crushed to make rich cooking oil. Every village has its own olive groves, with many containing gnarled trees that are centuries old.

Scents of the Maquis

Much of the terrain of Greece consists of a dense tangle of thorny shrubs known as *maquis*. Maquis plants thrive on stony ground throughout the mainland and islands. They can survive long periods of time without water.

ANCIENT FLOCKS

The island of Ródos near the Turkish coast is one of the few places left in Europe where farmers raise an ancient type of sheep called the mouflon. These reddish-brown animals have long, curving horns that the males use to fight with during the breeding season. Experts believe that all modern breeds of sheep are descended from this ancient species.

Nearby Crete has another rare relative of the mouflon: the *kri kri* or Cretan goat. These animals have lived on the island since Minoan times (Crete's ancient people) and now survive only in remote gorges and nature reserves.

▲ A Cretan goat perches on a steep, rocky slope.

They include glossy-leaved trees and shrubs such as holm oak, myrtle, and bay. Underfoot are herbs such as thyme, rosemary, and oregano, which give the maquis a strong, tangy scent—and the herbs featured in Greek cooking, too. The dense vegetation provides a habitat for nesting birds, such as larks and warblers.

▲ Pink geraniums grow beside the ruins of the Temple of Poseidon on Cape Sounion.

Bloom Time

In spring, Greece is filled with wildflowers. Bright splashes of red poppies and tall spikes of gladioli, lupin, and iris cover hillsides. Crocuses and delicate anemones bloom in shady woods. Greece is home to about 6,000 species of flowering plants, including many that are found nowhere else. The maquis is dotted with magenta-and-white rock roses and yellow fennel flowers.

▼ Night herons hunt for fish in Greece's freshwater wetlands and lakes.

FIRE SALAMANDER

The word *salamander* was the name of a "fire lizard" in a Greek legend. This mythical monster was probably inspired by the fire salamander, an amphibian found in the forests and mountains of Greece. Fire salamanders defend themselves using a poisonous fluid produced in special glands on their heads. They can squirt milky poison at attackers. If it gets in a person's eyes, the poison causes terrible stinging pains and sometimes heart problems. Fire salamanders have bright black and yellow markings to warn enemies that they are poisonous.

The wildflowers provide food for clouds of colorful butterflies. Reptiles such as Hermann's tortoise and the Ródos dragon, or large agama lizard, warm themselves on sunny rocks. Geckoes are often seen in villages. With their sticky toes, these acrobatic lizards dart across the ceilings in search of flies.

Mammal Life

Ancient writers speak of leopards and lions roaming the wilds of Greece. Those days are now long gone, but in remote areas you may still catch a glimpse of mammals that are very scarce elsewhere in Europe. Wolves and brown bears survive in parts of the Pindus and Rhodope Mountains. Brown bears eat both plants and animals. In fall, they feast on wild cherries. Wolves mostly eat meat like sheep. Shepherds keep fierce sheepdogs to guard their flocks against wolves. Wild boar, martens, red squirrels, crested porcupines, and badgers are found in Greek forests. Scrublands and pastures are home to wild cats and the occasional jackal pack or lynx.

Birdwatcher's Paradise

Greece is a good place to see birds any time of year. In spring, geese, ducks, and swallows stop by on their migration from Africa to northern Europe. In fall, the birds pass through again on their way south. Other birds stay in Greece all year, or arrive in fall to avoid the harsh northern winters. Birds of prey, including eagles, patrol remote uplands in search of rodents like mice and voles.

▲ The coastal waters of Greece are filled with wildlife, such as this starfish, as well as the remains of ancient civilizations.

Life in the Seas

Greece's long coastline and clear waters make it a great place to spot marine life. Spiny sea urchins, starfish, sea anemones, and sponges carpet the bed of clean coves. Delicate seahorses and their slender cousins, the pipefish, hide out in seaweed. Out at sea common and bottlenose dolphins sometimes swim alongside ships. Larger fish include blue and mako sharks.

VILLAGE TREES

In villages all over Greece, the lower trunks of trees are painted white (right). The color is chosen partly because it looks pretty, but the paint also has a practical purpose. It contains lime to fend off ants, which might harm the trees. The main square of most towns and villages in Greece contains at least one old and mighty tree that gives shade to local people. It may be a giant plane

tree, an oak, or a chestnut. Villages with names such as Kastania (chestnut) and Platanos (plane) are named after these trees.

Land of Empires

THE MODERN SKYLINE OF ATHENS is dominated by an ancient citadel called the Acropolis. This steep-sided, rocky outcrop is crowned by the soaring columns of a temple dedicated to the goddess Athena, the city's protector in ancient times (according to mythology). This ancient wonder dates back to the golden age of Greece, when the Greeks led the world in science, mathematics, and the arts.

In the 2nd century B.C., Greece was conquered by the Romans, which marked the start of 2,000 years of foreign rule. Standing on the Acropolis, you look down over Roman buildings and the winding streets of Plaka—a district built centuries ago during Turkish rule. In 1832, Greece won independence, and the modern state of Greece was born.

◀ The Parthenon, the main Acropolis building, was finished in 432 B.C. Many newer buildings have been knocked down to make the Parthenon clearly visible.

ONE LAND, MANY STATES

In ancient times, Greece was divided among small city-states. In 338 B.C. it came under Macedonian rule. By 146 B.C. it had been absorbed into the Roman Empire, which split into eastern and western halves in A.D. 395. Greece was part of the eastern half, the Byzantine Empire, for more than 1,000 years until it was taken over by the Turks in 1460. It remained under Turkish rule until it won independence in 1832. The new Greek state was small, made up only of the southern mainland, the Peloponnese, and the Sporades and

Cyclades. Gradually Greece enlarged its territory, reaching its present size in 1949.

▲ The city-states of ancient Greece had various systems of governments. Athens was ruled by the first democracy, in which the city's men gathered on a city hill to vote on important issues.

Time line

This chart shows some of the important dates in the history of Greece from the earliest civilizations in Crete to the present democratic republic.

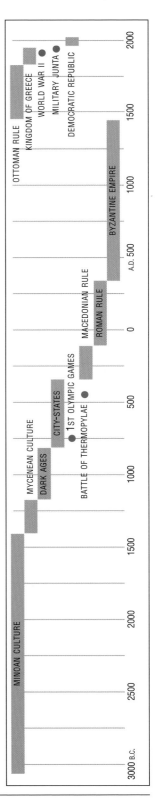

MINOAN CULTURE

MYCENEAN CULTURE

DARK AGES

CITY-STATES

● 1ST OLYMPIC GAMES

BATTLE OF THERMOPYLAE ●

MACEDONIAN RULE

ROMAN RULE

BYZANTINE EMPIRE

OTTOMAN RULE

KINGDOM OF GREECE

WORLD WAR II ●

MILITARY JUNTA ●

DEMOCRATIC REPUBLIC

3000 B.C.   2500   2000   1500   1000   500   0   A.D. 500   1000   1500   2000

Historical Map

MAP KEY

Minoan ca 2900–1150 B.C.

Mycenaean ca 1400–1100 B.C.

Mycenaean ca 750–323 B.C.

◆ Bronze Age sites

◆ Minoan sites

◆ Mycenaean sites

◆ Classical sites

● Selected present-day city

Present-day boundaries, drainage, and place names are shown.

ITALY

SICILY

Ionian Sea

ALBANIA

MACEDONIA

Danube

Black Sea

TURKEY

Byzantium
(Istanbul) ●

Aegean Sea

BATTLE SCENE,
page 29

Pátra ●

Mycenae

Olympia

GOLDEN MASK,
page 26

☐ *Thermopylae*

Thebes

CAVALRY BATTLE,
page 32

Athens

Corinth

Sparta

ISLAND FORTRESS,
page 30

Thíra
(Santorini)

FLOODLIT ANCIENT BUILDING,
pages 2–3, 22–23,
AND
THEATER PERFORMANCE,
page 28
AND
STATUE,
page 31
AND
DOMED CHURCH,
page 31
AND
TANKS IN STREET,
page 33

Sea of Crete

Haniá ●

Iráklio ● Knossos

Crete

RUINED PALACE,
page 26

Mediterranean Sea

Cyprus ◆

0   miles   200

0   km   200

Early Civilizations

The first great civilization in Greece was the Minoan culture, which reached a peak in about 2000 B.C. Based in Crete, the Minoans were great seafarers and merchants and built an empire through trade. Wall paintings found in the ruined palace at Knossos show scenes from Minoan life. They include ceremonies in which young people took turns doing backflips over a charging bull. The bull was sacred to the Minoans. Around 1450 B.C. the Minoans were conquered by the Myceneans, a warlike people from mainland Greece.

▲ This palace at Knossos was the center of Minoan civilization.

▼ This Mycenean death mask is known as "the face of Agamemnon" for the king who started the Trojan War.

The Myceneans ruled from fortified cities. Theirs was the age of heroes and warriors, later celebrated by the poet Homer in his epic poem, *The Iliad*. Homer tells of a war between the Greeks and the Trojans, caused by the kidnapping of a Greek queen named Helen. The Greeks besieged the city of Troy (now an archaeological site in Turkey) for ten years. They finally tricked their way into the city by hiding in the body of a giant wooden horse.

By 1100 B.C., the Mycenean

civilization had collapsed and their cities were abandoned. The next several centuries were Greece's Dark Ages. People lived in small villages but aspects of Mycenean culture and religion remained. Greek gods were believed to live on Mount Olympus. Zeus was king of gods and ruled the heavens. His brothers reigned over the rest of the Universe: Poseidon ruled the sea, while Hades was the god of the underworld. Zeus's son Apollo was god of the Sun, while his daughter Athena was goddess of wisdom.

Rise of City-States

In the eighth century B.C., a new age dawned. City-states such as Athens, Sparta, Thebes, and Corinth

BIRTH OF THE OLYMPICS

The original Olympic Games was a sporting festival held every four years in honor of Zeus, the king of the gods. The first games were held at Olympia in southern Greece in the 700s B.C. In times of war, states declared a truce so their athletes could take part. Only men were allowed to enter. Events such as sprinting, long jump, discus, javelin, and wrestling are still part of the modern games. Other sports such as chariot racing do not take place today. One of the most popular events would never be allowed in the modern games. The *pankration* was the ultimate fighting sport. There were no weight classes, no time limits, and only two rules: no biting and no eye gouging. The losers were often badly injured. In A.D. 393 the Olympic games were banned by the Romans. They were revived in their modern form in Athens in 1896.

▲ In the Hoplite event, competitors raced in full armor. Each Olympic winner was awarded a crown of olive leaves.

began to grow. Each state controlled territory around a single city. The ancient Greek word for a city—*polis*—is the root of words such as *politics* and *metropolis*.

The Greek states were frequently at war with one another, but occasionally they united to fight a common enemy, such as the Persians. By the fifth century B.C., Athens had become the most powerful city-state.

New Ideas

The next 200 years were the golden age of ancient Greece. New branches of art and learning developed. Students today still study the work of ancient Greek thinkers, such as the philosopher Aristotle and the mathematician Euclid.

Most Greek city-states were ruled by noblemen, but in 508 B.C., Athens introduced a new system called

A TOUGH TOWN

Sparta, in southern Greece, was Athens's main rival. Sparta was not a place for the weak. All babies were checked by the city elders, and infants considered weak were left to die on a hillside. Boys were sent to military camp at the age of seven. They trained as warriors under harsh military discipline—they were even starved so that they would steal food and learn to be cunning! As a result the Spartans had a reputation for being tough. In one legendary battle, 300 Spartans held off many thousands of Persian troops at Thermopylae in 480 B.C. Recently this story has been retold in the movie *300*.

▲ The 300 Spartans held back the Persian army for three days before being defeated.

democracy—rule by the people. Modern countries have governments inspired by this first democracy. However, unlike today, only men could vote in Athens.

Foreign Rule

In 338 B.C., Philip II of Macedonia took control of Greece. When he was assassinated two years later, his son took over. Within 13 years Alexander had carved

ALEXANDER THE GREAT

In a country of great leaders, Alexander of Macedonia was the greatest. He became king at the age of just 20 in 336 B.C. He set out to conquer the mighty Persian Empire. Marching south and east, his armies built an empire that stretched into Egypt and east through Persia (now Iran and Afghanistan) to India. There, Alexander (right) was forced to turn back when his battle-weary troops rebelled. He founded many cities in the lands he had conquered. When he died of a fever in 323 B.C., his empire was divided among his generals. Much of the territory he won remained under Greek rule for another 200 years.

SPOILS OF HOLY WAR

I n the 12th and 13th centuries Christian soldiers from western Europe, called Crusaders, began a series of religious wars in the "Holy Land"—the region of West Asia around Jerusalem that had been home to Jesus Christ. Most Crusaders wanted to take the area away from its Muslim rulers. However, some were just out to get land and grow rich. In 1204, soldiers from Venice (now in Italy) invaded Greece. By the 1270s, Byzantine forces had recaptured much of Greece, but Crete and the Ionian Islands remained in Venetian hands for hundreds of years afterward.

▲ The island fortress of Bourdzi was built by Venetians in southern Greece in the 1300s.

out an empire stretching all the way to India. Although the Romans conquered the country by 146 B.C., they still revered ancient Greece. Roman nobles sent their sons to be educated in Athens.

By A.D. 330, the Romans were losing control of their vast empire. Emperor Constantine built a new capital in the east at Byzantium, which he renamed Constantinople (present-day Istanbul in Turkey). Soon after, the eastern Roman Empire, including Greece, broke from the west, becoming the Byzantine Empire.

The Byzantine Empire survived long after the fall of the Western Empire based in Rome. However, during the 1200s Byzantine power was weakened by a series of religious wars known as the Crusades. By 1460, Greece had become part of the vast Ottoman Empire, ruled by Muslim Turks from the east.

A POET AND HERO

During the 1820s, the Greeks had a lot of support from other European nations in their fight for independence from the Turks. Lovers of ancient Greek culture traveled to Greece to join this revolution, including the English poet Lord Byron, famous for his long poem *Don Juan*. Lame from birth but very handsome, Byron had many love affairs and was described as "mad, bad, and dangerous to know." He was made an officer in the Greek army, but soon died of a fever. His death increased support for the Greek cause. Britain, France, and Russia sent forces that defeated the Turks at the Battle of Navarino. Byron is still honored as a Greek hero.

▲ A statue of Byron in Athens shows him worshipping Greece—depicted as a woman.

The Fight for Independence

The Ottomans allowed their Greek subjects to keep their culture and follow their own Orthodox Christian religion. However, by the 1700s, many Greeks were unhappy with being ruled by foreigners. In 1821, a full-scale war broke out against the Turks. The Greeks won

▼ Some Greek buildings, such as this church in Athens, are still built in the Byzantine style.

in 1829, thanks to help from other European armies. The modern state of Greece was officially founded in 1832, although it was only about half its present size. The first king of Greece, King Otto, was hand picked by the European allies. He was a member of a German noble family and was just 17 years old when he took the throne. Otto was not popular, and his 30-year reign was a time of great instability in Greek history.

The Great Idea

Greece began a series of wars to increase its territory to include all the lands where Greek people lived. This was called the "Great Idea." The country expanded northward to include Thessaly, Macedonia, and Epirus. In 1908, Crete also chose to become part of Greece. Greek armies then headed east into Turkey, but were finally defeated in 1922. More than a million Greeks living in western Turkey were forced to resettle in Greece, which increased the population by a quarter and caused major economic problems.

▼ Greek cavalry charges at a battle at Smyrna in 1922. Smyrna is called Izmir today and is a part of Turkey.

GREECE SAYS NO

In 1940 at the start of World War II, Italian leader Benito Mussolini demanded that the Greek government allow Italian troops to pass through Greece. Greek leader Ioannis Metaxas's answer was a single word: "Óhi!"—"no" in Greek. With this one word Greece entered the war on the side of the Allies. As a result, Italian and German forces invaded. Every October 28, Greeks celebrate Óhi Day to remember Greece's resistance.

▲ German tanks roll through Athens as Greece is invaded in 1941.

Continuing Unrest

In the 1930s, there were growing calls to change the system of government. In 1936 Ioannis Metaxas took control of Greece. He allowed the king to stay but ruled as a dictator. During World War II (1939–1945), Greece was occupied by Italian, German, and Bulgarian troops. The country was freed in 1944, and the king was restored. However, civil war broke out between royalists and communists. Government forces won in 1949. In 1967, a group of military officers seized power. The king fled to Italy.

In 1974 democracy was restored. Greeks voted against having a king and made their country a republic. In 1981, Greece joined the European Union (EU).

▼ Constantine II was the last king of Greece. He ruled with his wife Princess Anne-Marie of Denmark from 1964 to 1974. He was in exile for most of his reign.

Friends
and
Family

THE *KAFENEIO*, OR COFFEE SHOP, is the focus of social life in Greece. You will find one in every village square and on most city streets. People sit at tables, swapping gossip, talking politics, or playing backgammon. You may hear a clicking sound as worry beads are idly flipped over. Worry beads look like rosary beads, but they have no religious meaning—they are just something to play with. The kafeneio's customers are mostly men, but anyone is allowed in. Greeks are famous for their hospitality and friendliness to strangers. The Greek word for "foreigner"—*xenós*—also means "guest." Greece has modernized a lot in recent years, but like many other traditions, the custom of being kind to strangers remains strong.

◄ Greeks take a rest from the day's activities at the local kafeneio. In addition to coffee, the kafeneio serves simple food, including lamb stews and cheese salads.

THE PEOPLE OF GREECE

About 93 percent of people living in Greece regard themselves as Greek. The other 7 percent of the population includes Albanians, Turks, Slavs (from Serbia), Vlachs (from Romania), and Roma (or Gypsies). Albanians are the biggest minority. Most left their country in the 1990s to find work abroad. Today they form around 15 percent of Greece's workforce. In the 1950s and 1960s, many thousands of Greeks also left to work abroad. Many went to North America and Australia. Melbourne, Australia, has half a million Greek residents and it is jokingly described as being Greece's third-biggest city! During the same period many Greeks also moved into cites. In 1950, less than half the population lived in cities—now nearly two-thirds of Greeks do.

▼ **A Greek man dressed in traditional clothes during a village festival**

Common Greek Phrases

Here are a few Greek phrases to try. They are shown here in the Western alphabet but are normally written in Greek letters.

Good morning	Kalimera	ka-lih-MEH-ra
Good evening	Kalispéra	ka-lih-SPEH-ra
Thank you	Efharistó	ef-HAH-rih-STOH
How are you?	Ti kánete?	ti KAH-neh-teh
I am fine	Íme kalá	IH-meh ka-LAH
Yes	Ne	neh
No	Óhi	O-hee
Please	Parakaló	pah-rah-kah-LOH

1950 / 7.6 million	1970 / 8.8 million
37% urban / 63% rural	53% urban / 47% rural

1990 / 10.1 million	2005 / 11.1 million
59% urban / 41% rural	61% urban / 39% rural

BULGARIA

MACEDONIA

ALBANIA

TURKEY

Mediterranean Sea

Aegean Sea

Sea of Crete

Ionian Sea

Orestiáda

Komotiní

Xánthi

Dráma

Séres

Kaválá

Alexandroúpoli

Kilkís

Thessaloníki
(Salonica)

Kalamariá

Katerini

Gianitsá

Véroia

Édessa

Flórina

Náousa

Kastoriá

Ptolemaída

Kozáni

Ioánnina

Trikala

Lárissa

Kardítsa

Árta

Vólos

Mitilíni

Halkída

Néa Ionía

Livadiá

Thíva

Lamía

Préveza

Agrínio

Kérkira

Náfpaktos

Pátra

Égio

Kórinthos
(Corinth)

Athens

Argos

Amaliáda

Pírgos

Trípoli

Spárti

Kalamáta

Híos

Kos

Ródos

Iráklio

Haniá

Réthimno

CLIFFTOP MONASTERY,
page 45

COFFEE SHOP,
pages 3; 34–35

CITY STREET,
page 38
AND

OLIVE SELLER,
page 40
AND

MARATHON RUNNERS,
page 43,
AND

WOMEN DIVERS,
page 43

MAN IN TRADITIONAL
GREEK DRESS,
page 36

RELIGIOUS
PROCESSION,
page 45

WEDDING
CEREMONY,
page 39

GIRL WEARING
GOLDEN NECKLACE,
page 39

MUSICIANS PLAYING
TRADITIONAL INSTRUMENTS,
page 44

**People per
square mile**

**People per
square kilometer**

Over 2500 — Over 1000

626–2499 — 250–999

61–625 — 25–249

12–60 — 5–24

Under 12 — Under 5

Population of urban area

■ Over 500,000

▲ 100,000 to 500,000

● 50,000 to 100,000

• Under 50,000

miles — 0 ... 100

km — 0 ... 100

▲ Although Athens is an ancient city, it is still very much alive. Around the Acropolis and other ancient sites, Athenians carry on their lives on the busy streets and in crowded apartment buildings.

Country and City

Since the 1950s, hundreds of thousands of Greeks have moved from rural areas to cities in search of better work and a more comfortable life. As a result, Greece's cities have expanded beyond recognition. Athens was home to 700,000 citizens in 1950 and now has 3.7 million people. There is a shortage of housing, so families have to crowd into small apartments. The busy roads also produce a lot of pollution. Car fumes react with the strong sunlight to produce smog, called *nefos* in Greek. It is sometimes so bad that it gives people breathing problems. Traffic is now restricted in the center of Athens to keep the air clear.

The pace of life is faster in cities than the countryside. However, in both town and country, life comes to a halt in mid-afternoon, when people take a rest to avoid the hottest time of day. All stores and banks close for a few hours and open again in the early evening.

Being Together

The family is important in Greek life. Relatives often live close together—sometimes in next-door apartments. Young Greek people do not always get their own apartments. They live with their parents, even after they get married. Sometimes families add a floor or new addition to their home when a son or daughter gets married and starts a family. It is common to see many buildings that look unfinished. In fact, they are topped with a layer of concrete so that they are ready for a new floor to be added. A young couple stays with one set of parents until they have enough money to get a place of their own—somewhere nearby.

NATIONAL HOLIDAYS

Many national holidays in Greece are also Christian feast days. For example, Independence Day is also the Feast of the Annunciation. It is celebrated with dances and family meals. On Labor Day, families also eat picnics outdoors and watch parades. The country's main holidays are Easter, Christmas, and Assumption, which remembers the death of the Virgin Mary.

JAN 1	New Year's Day
MARCH 25	Independence Day
MARCH/APRIL	Easter
MAY 1	Labor Day
AUGUST 15	Assumption
OCTOBER 28	Óhi Day
DECEMBER 25	Christmas

▶ During an Easter ceremony, Greek girls dress in ornate clothing and wear necklaces of gold coins.

▼ At a Greek wedding, a couple is showered with rice by their friends and families.

A NATIONAL DISH

Every part of Greece has its own version of *horiátiki,* or "village salad." The name comes from *horío,* Greek for village. The basics are tomato, cucumber, and slices of feta—cheese made from sheep's milk. Olives, onions, peppers, capers, and lettuce may be added. The mixture is dressed with vinegar and olive oil. Horiátiki is eaten as a snack or to accompany a main dish. Other delicious Greek snacks include *souvlaki*—lamb grilled on a skewer—and *tiropita* and *spanakopita*—cheese and spinach pies.

Eating in Greece

Greeks are often up early in the morning and eat a simple breakfast of bread, honey, and cheese. They eat lunch and dinner later than in many other countries in order to fit around the afternoon rest period. A large meal usually begins with a mixture of appetizers, or *mezédes.* These include olives, hummus (a paste made from chickpeas, sesame seeds, and olive oil), and refreshing tzatziki (a mixture of yogurt and cucumber). This is served with pita bread.

Greeks eat a lot of meat, especially lamb. One of the most famous dishes is moussaka: layers of baked ground lamb and slices of eggplant.

▼ **A market trader sells a selection of green and black olives in Athens.**

Seafoods such as fish, squid, and octopus are also popular. The eggs, or roe, of carp riverfish are mixed with lemon juice, olive oil, and garlic to make a delicious dip called taramasalata.

Greeks also eat a lot of fresh fruit, and vegetables cooked in olive oil and served warm. With this

▲ Sardines are hung on a line to dry in the sun.

healthy and varied diet, it is no wonder that Greeks live long lives compared with people from most other countries. Men live to an average age of 77 and women have a life expectancy of 82.

Going to School

The state provides free education for all Greek children between the ages of six and 15. After six years of primary school, children go to a secondary school, called a *gymnasium*. Some students end their educations at age 15, while others go on to three more years at a *lykeion*, or high school. Then students may go on to study at a university in one of the big cities.

Many small islands have no secondary schools. Students take a ferry to a neighboring island each morning, or their parents send their children to live with a relative on the mainland until they finish their schooling. The school day is shorter in Greece than in

ANCIENT INSIGHTS

Ancient Greek thinkers were the first Europeans to think about philosophy, math, and science—and they made many discoveries. The doctor Hippocrates introduced a scientific approach to medicine. Doctors today swear to follow a code of conduct called the Hippocratic Oath. The mathematician Pythagoras is famous for his theorem about the sides of triangles. He was also among the first to suggest that the world was round, not flat. The astronomer Aristarchos of Samos also said that the Earth moved around the Sun, not the other way around, while Democritus described how everything was made of tiny atoms. And the scientist Archimedes first explained volume and density. According to legend, he discovered this while in the bath. He rushed into the street naked, shouting "Eureka," meaning "I have it!"

▲ Archimedes used his discoveries to check how much gold was in the king's crown.

other countries, but after school children may have private lessons in music or a foreign language.

One Nation, Two Languages

Ancient Greek was quite different from the language spoken in modern Greece. For a long time, there were two versions of modern Greek: *katharevousa* and *dimotikí*. Katharevousa was the formal language used for official documents, such as laws. It is closer to ancient Greek than dimotikí, or demotic—the language of everyday speech. Today, the differences between the two forms of Greek are almost gone.

The importance of Greek learning to Western culture is reflected in the many scientific and technical words in English and other languages that come from ancient Greek. Words ending in -*graphy*, such as *geography*, come from the Greek word meaning "to write." Geography, therefore, means writing about the Earth. Words that end in -*logy*, such as *biology*, come from the Greek *logos*, meaning "word." Biology literally means "words about life."

Fun and Games

Soccer and basketball are the most popular sports in Greece. Water sports, such as swimming and sailing, are also popular, as are volleyball and track sports.

In 2004, the Olympic Games were held in Athens. Track-and-field events at the games, such as running, javelin, and discus, date back to the ancient Olympic Games. The distance of a marathon (26 miles; 42 km) is based on the distance from Athens to Marathon. According to legend, in 490 B.C. a messenger called Pheidippides ran from Athens to Marathon to get news of a battle against the Persians. He then ran all the way back to announce Athens's victory. Then poor Pheidippides dropped dead!

▲ Marathon runners pass a statue of Pheidippides during the Athens Olympic Games in 2004.

▼ Greek divers compete at the European Championships.

Time to Relax

On weekends and in the evenings, Greeks like to socialize in cafés and tavernas (restaurants). Greek families take their time eating. Dinner is served as late as 10:00 P.M., and even young children are allowed to stay up.

▲ Musicians play bouzoukis at a village wedding celebration.

As people eat, there is usually music playing. Traditional Greek music is very distinctive and is popular with young and old: Pop and rock music have not replaced it yet! The main instrument is a long-necked lute called a bouzouki. As the meal ends, late in the night, people will move the tables aside so they can dance—often traditional dances.

Community Action

Religion is a strong force in modern Greece. An overwhelming 98 percent of the population is Greek Orthodox—the eastern branch of Christianity that developed during Byzantine times. There are also a few Muslims—1.3 percent of the population, mostly from Turkey—and smaller numbers of Roman Catholics, Protestants, and Jews. Greek Orthodox priests are all men. They wear tall black hats and flowing robes and many also have beards.

MEN-ONLY MOUNTAIN

Mount Athos, the Holy Mountain, stands on a peninsula in northern Greece. This community of Orthodox Christian monks is a tiny self-governing region. About a thousand years ago, the mountain was home to around 40 monasteries. Today, 20 are still in use. About 1,700 monks live on Mount Athos, but women have not been allowed in since A.D. 1060. Not even female animals are allowed!

▶ The Simonopetra Monastery, built on Mount Athos 700 years ago, looks out across the Aegean Sea.

On Sundays, churches are often full. Traditionally, this is a time for village women to meet and catch up on the news. A church service may last up to three hours, but people do not have to stay for the whole thing.

The biggest church festival of the year is Easter. City folk return to their home village. There are processions on Good Friday and Easter Saturday. Every village also has a patron saint, whose feast day is celebrated with another procession, a feast, fireworks, music, and dancing late into the night.

▼ The remains of a saint are carried over sick women who want to cure their illnesses.

Countries of the World: Greece

Marching
Back to
Greatness

THE GREEK PARLIAMENT, or Vouli, stands on Syntagma Square in Athens. Originally built as a royal palace, the parliament building has been the government's home since 1935. It is protected by the Evzones, or National Guard. These elite soldiers arrive on duty in traditional dress, which includes a kilt and red beret.

Greece is a rich country compared with its nearest neighbors in the Balkans, but poor compared to many Western nations. The country has only enjoyed peace and stability since the mid-1970s, which has allowed time for the economy to prosper. In recent years the economy has grown rapidly, but in some rural areas, village life has changed very little.

◀ **A member of the Evzones stands guard in Syntagma Square. Their uniform is based on the outfits worn by rebels during the fight for independence in the 1820s.**

REGIONS OF GREECE

The Greek mainland is divided into seven political regions, with Macedonia and Thrace forming the north and Epirus and Thessaly just below. The southeast of central Greece is Attica, the area surrounding Athens. The Peloponnese lies in the south. The final region is made up of the main groups of islands: the Ionians, Sporades, North Aegeans, Dodecanese, and Cyclades. In terms of local government, Greece is divided into 51 districts called *nomoi*, each of which is headed by a governor, or *nomarch*. The districts are divided into 147 smaller districts. Each city, town, and village has its own council. The one exception is Mount Athos, which is a self-governing community.

Trading Partners

Greece joined the European Union (EU) in 1981. This link with other European nations has been vital to the country's trade. About half of all Greece's trade is with other EU nations. Greece's exports include cement, chemicals, clothing and textiles, and processed foods, especially olive oil. Its most important imports are high-tech machinery, fuels, vehicles, and chemicals.

Country	Percent Greece exports
Germany	11.4%
Italy	10.7%
Cyprus	6.5%
Bulgaria	6.4%
All others combined	65.0%

Country	Percent Greece imports
Germany	12.9%
Italy	11.7%
Russia	5.6%
France	5.6%
All others combined	64.2%

▼ Containers are stacked on a wharf at Piraeus, Greece's largest port, located in Attica.

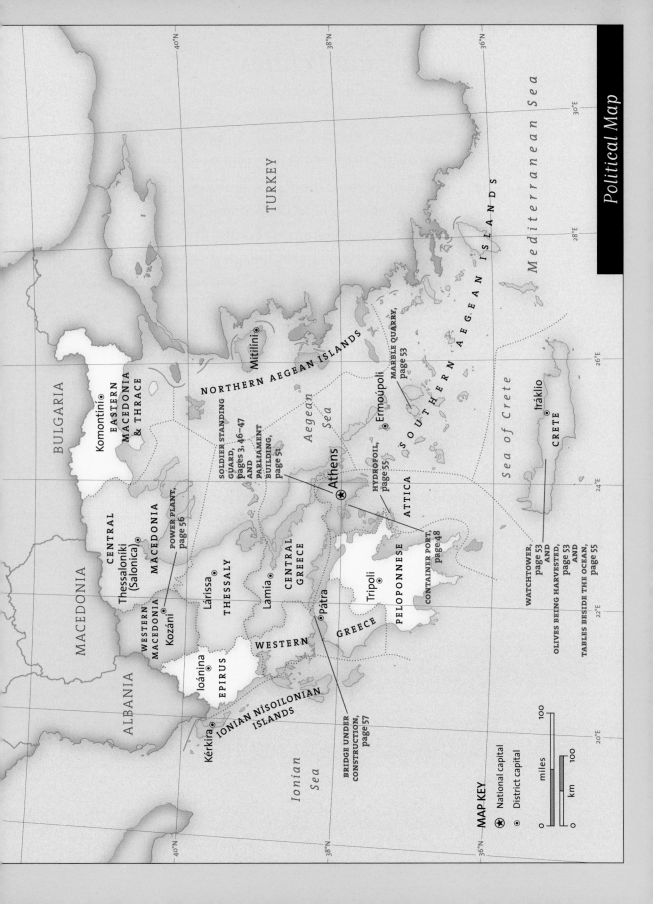

Political Map

MAP KEY

⊛ National capital
◉ District capital

0   miles   100

0   km   100

Ionian Sea

ALBANIA

MACEDONIA

IONIAN NÍSOI IONIAN
ISLANDS

Kérkira ◉

EPIRUS

Ioánina ◉

WESTERN
MACEDONIA

Kozáni ◉

CENTRAL
MACEDONIA

Thessaloníki
(Salonica) ◉

BULGARIA

Komontiní ◉

EASTERN
MACEDONIA
& THRACE

POWER PLANT,
page 56

THESSALY

Lárissa ◉

Lamía ◉

CENTRAL
GREECE

WESTERN
GREECE

Pátra ◉

BRIDGE UNDER
CONSTRUCTION, page 57

PELOPONNESE

Trípoli ◉

CONTAINER PORT,
page 48

Athens ⊛

ATTICA

HYDROFOIL,
page 55

SOLDIER STANDING
GUARD, pages 3, 46–47
AND
PARLIAMENT
BUILDING, page 51

Aegean Sea

NORTHERN AEGEAN ISLANDS

Mitilíni ◉

TURKEY

Ermoúpoli ◉

S O U T H E R N   A E G E A N   I S L A N D S

MARBLE QUARRY,
page 53

Sea of Crete

Iráklio ◉

CRETE

Mediterranean Sea

WATCHTOWER,
page 53
AND
OLIVES BEING HARVESTED,
page 53
AND
TABLES BESIDE THE OCEAN,
page 55

40°N
38°N
36°N

20°E
22°E
24°E
26°E
28°E
30°E

The Usual Politics

Politics is a Greek word. It means "art of government." Although the idea of democracy existed in ancient Greece, the modern country became a full democracy in the mid-1970s. Since then it has been dominated by two main parties: the Panhellenic Socialist Movement (PASOK) and the New Democracy. PASOK traditionally favors strong government control of the economy to ensure that the country's wealth is shared equally. PASOK has been in power for the majority of the last 30 years. The New Democracy party favors a free-market economy and believes that Greek people need to be able to look after themselves. New Democracy

HOW THE GOVERNMENT WORKS

Greece's constitution was written in 1975, following the fall of the military government. At that time Greeks voted to abolish the monarchy, and Greece became a republic. The state is headed by a president, but this role is mostly ceremonial. Real power lies with the prime minister, who heads the government. He or she is usually the leader of the party with the most seats in parliament. The prime minister selects a cabinet of ministers who head the various government departments. The Greek parliament, the Vouli, has only one house, with 300 members who are elected every four years. The highest court is the Special Supreme Court. Its 11 members are drawn from the heads of the lower criminal, financial, and civil courts.

GOVERNMENT		
EXECUTIVE	LEGISLATIVE	JUDICIARY
PRESIDENT	PRIME MINISTER	SPECIAL SUPREME COURT (CONSTITUTIONAL COURT)
CABINET OF MINISTERS	VOULI (300 MEMBERS)	COURT OF CASSATION (CRIMINAL COURT)

took power in the 2004 election. Its leader, Prime Minister Kostas Karamanlis, is the nephew of the party's founder, Konstantinos Karamanlis.

In the Neighborhood

One of the issues commonly debated in Greek coffee shops is Greece's relations with its neighbors. After nearly four centuries of Ottoman rule and the forced exchange of populations in the 1920s, Greece has a troubled relationship with Turkey. Other flashpoints between the two nations include the Dodecanese Islands, which are owned by Greece but are just a few miles from Turkey, and the Mediterranean island of Cyprus, which is home to both Greek and Turkish communities.

In the 1990s a crisis exploded with another neighbor. Until 1991, Greece shared a border with the state of Yugoslavia. That year, Yugoslavia began to break up into smaller republics. One was Macedonia, which borders Greece. The region of Greece next to this country is also called Macedonia. The Greeks feared that the new republic might one day call for all

▲ Kostas Karamanlis, the current prime minister of Greece, greets supporters at a rally.

▼ Greek protests often end at the steps of the Vouli, the Greek parliament. A major riot took place there in 2008 in protest of police brutality.

DISPUTED ISLAND

The island of Cyprus in the eastern Mediterranean Sea is mostly populated by Greeks but also has a large Turkish community. The island won independence from Britain in 1960. In 1974, the army officers who ruled Greece at the time overthrew the Cypriot leader. Turkish troops arrived to prevent a complete takeover by Greece and occupied the northern third of the island. War was narrowly avoided, but many Greeks were forced out of the Turkish area. The crisis brought about the downfall of the Greek junta. The island is still divided into Greek and Turkish areas, and despite peace talks with the EU, the situation has not yet been resolved.

▲ United Nations soldiers from around the world take turns guarding the border to make sure Greek and Turkish forces do not fight over Cyprus.

Macedonians—including those in Greece—to be united as one country. The European Union and United Nations came up with a solution. The new republic is now known as FYR Macedonia—the Former Yugoslav Republic of Macedonia.

Farming and Fishing

Before 1950 most people in Greece earned a living by either farming or fishing. Despite Greece's poor soil, most families lived off a small plot of land. They harvested olives for oil and grapes for wine, and raised sheep or goats for milk, cheese, meat, and wool. At the end of each year there was little left to sell.

Most modern farms are run on a commercial basis, growing crops for export. The main crops grown are

wheat, cotton, maize, tobacco, citrus fruits, tomatoes, vegetables, olives, and grapes.

On coasts and islands, people traditionally lived by fishing. You still see fishermen mending their yellow nets. However, the industry has suffered from overfishing. So many fish have been caught in Greek waters that many species are now rare. Fish-farming is a growing business, with sea bream and bass raised for local restaurants and sale abroad.

▲ Greece is known for its ancient marble buildings. Marble is still quarried in the country for export.

▼ Even today Greek olives are often harvested by hand.

Making Money
About a fifth of Greek workers are employed in manufacturing, an industry that makes up about a quarter of the country's income. Greek factories produce cement,

INDUSTRY AND MINING

This map shows the location of Greece's most important mines and industrial areas. Most industry is based either in Athens or Thessaloniki, the second-largest city. Greece's most important mineral is lignite, a form of brown coal. Large deposits of lignite lie in the Pindus Mountains, the island of Évia, and the Peloponnese. Bauxite is mined to make aluminum, and chromite is used for stainless steel. There are also reserves of barite, iron ore, lead, zinc, and magnesite. Limestone is used for cement. Greece ranks second after China in world cement production. Fine marble is also quarried on the island of Paros.

o — mi — 100
o — km — 100

Thessaloníki (Salonica)

Lg
Cr
Lg
Pb Zn

Cr
Bx
Al
Bx
Ni
Mg

Aegean Sea

Fe
Athens

Ionian Sea

MAP KEY
* Manufacturing center
◖ Cement

Major Mines
Al Aluminium   Fe Iron ore   Mg Magnesium
Bx Bauxite   Pb Lead   Ni Nickel
Cr Chromite   Lg Lignite   Zn Zinc

Mediterranean Sea

chemicals, cigarettes, shoes, clothing, paper, rubber goods, and processed food and drink.

Top Industries

Over two-thirds of Greeks work in service industries, which include banking, government services, schools, transportation, hospitals, and tourism.

Tourism makes up about 15 percent of the nation's economy. It is also a source of foreign currency, which makes it easier to buy things made abroad. The same number of people visit Greece each year as actually live there. Tourists come to enjoy the fine beaches or to visit ancient sites.

Athens is the single most popular attraction, followed by the ancient sites of Corinth, Épidaurus, Olympia, Mycenae, Delphi, and the Byzantine village of Mistras. Popular islands for a beach vacation include Kérkira, Crete, Mikonos, Ródos, and Thíra (Santorini). Many tourists explore several islands by ferry—an activity called "island-hopping."

Tourism is a major employer, with many thousands of Greeks working in hotels, restaurants, or shops, working as guides, or running ferries, buses, and other transportation. Tourism is usually confined to the summer, but the Ministry of Tourism is taking steps to promote Greece as a year-round destination. The rapid expansion of tourism has created a few problems. Some islands have been overdeveloped, which causes problems for wildlife. In the summer, large numbers of visitors can lead to water shortages on some islands.

▲ With such a long coast, Greece has many seaside vacation resorts.

▼ Hydrofoils provide high-speed links between Greek islands and the mainland.

Greek Power

In 1960 less than half of all homes in Greece had electricity. Now only the most remote villages are without it. Greece's main source of fuel is a low-grade coal called lignite. The country has very little of its own oil and gas, and so must import

what it needs. About 10 percent of Greece's electricity comes from hydroelectric plants on mountain rivers. Greece has great potential for renewable forms of energy, such as wind and solar power. Small solar panels can be seen on roofs throughout Greece, but no large solar plants have been built because they are too expensive. Windmills have been used to generate energy since ancient times, and there are a number of modern wind farms being built.

▼ Thick smoke belches from the Aghios Dimitrios power plant in northern Greece. The plant burns lignite, a type of coal mined nearby. Protesters say that the Greek plant is Europe's most polluting power plant.

To the Future

Greece's economy is still developing. Between 2000 and 2006, it received $8 billion in aid each year from the European Union. From 2007 to 2013, it will receive $3.8 billion a year. The government hopes economic progress will continue, even though its aid is now reduced.

One of Greece's problems is balancing its imports and exports. The total value of all the goods it imports far outweighs the value of its exports. The Greek government aims to tackle this by starting new industries and making existing ones more efficient. Like many countries, it has also had to wrestle with unemployment and

56   Countries of the World: Greece

THE ONASSIS FAMILY

Greece's super-rich shipping tycoons are world famous. They control about a fifth of the world's cargo ships and ferries. The most famous dynasty is the Onassis family, whose fortune was made by Aristotle Onassis. Originally based in Smyrna (now Izmir, Turkey), the Onassis family fled to Athens during World War I. Aristotle then went to Argentina and became rich as a farmer and ship owner. In 1946 he married Athina Livanos, the daughter of another Greek shipping baron. The couple had two children, Alexander and Christina, before divorcing. Onassis's second wife was Jacqueline Kennedy, widow of U.S. president John F. Kennedy. In 1973, Alexander Onassis died in a plane crash. Aristotle Onassis died two years later, leaving more than $2 billion to Christina. However, she died in 1988, leaving the Onassis fortune in the hands of Athina Onassis Roussel, her three-year-old daughter.

▲ Athina Onassis Roussel, the granddaughter of Aristotle Onassis, visits Athens in 1998 with her father Thiery. Today, she lives in Argentina.

immigration. Since the 1980s, Greek towns and cities have modernized quickly, but rural areas have lagged behind. Standards of living have improved, bringing Greece more in line with western Europe. There is considerable optimism, particularly among young Greeks, who have much greater opportunities than their parents and grandparents enjoyed.

▼ The Rio-Antirio bridge, under construction in 2004, was built across the Gulf of Corinth to carry a highway to the Peloponnese.

Add a Little Extra to Your Country Report!

If you are assigned to write a report about Greece, you'll want to include basic information about the country, of course. The Fast Facts chart on page 8 will give you a good start. The rest of the book will give you the details you need to create a full and up-to-date paper or PowerPoint presentation. But what can you do to make your report more fun than anyone else's? If you use your imagination and dig a bit deeper into some of the topics introduced in this book, you're sure to come up with information that will make your report unique!

>Flag

Perhaps you could explain the history of Greece's flag and the meanings of its colors and symbols. Go to **www.crwflags.com/fotw/ flags** for more information.

>National Anthem

How about downloading Greece's national anthem and playing it for your class? At **www.nationalanthems.info** you'll find what you need, including the words to the anthem, plus sheet music for it. Simply pick "G" and then "Greece" from the list on the left-hand side of the screen, and you're on your way.

>Time Difference

If you want to understand the time difference between Greece and where you are, this Web site can help: **www.worldtimeserver.com**. Just pick "Greece" from the list on the left. If you called someone in Greece right now, would you wake them up from their sleep?

>*Currency*

Another Web site will convert your money into euros, the currency used in Greece. You'll want to know how much money to bring if you're lucky enough to travel to Greece: **www.xe.com/ucc**.

>*Weather*

Why not check the current weather in Greece? It's easy—go to **www.weather.com** to find out if it's sunny or cloudy, warm, or cold in Greece right now! Pick "World" from the headings at the top of the page. Then search for Greece. Click on any city. Be sure to click on the tabs below the weather report for Sunrise/Sunset information, Weather Watch, and Business Travel Outlook, too. Scroll down the page for the 36-Hour Forecast and a satellite weather map. Compare your weather to the weather in the Greek city you chose. Is this a good season, weather-wise, for a person to travel to Greece?

>*Miscellaneous*

Still want more information? Simply go to National Geographic's World Atlas for Young Explorers at **http://www.nationalgeographic.com/ kids-world-atlas**. It will help you find maps, photos, music, games, and other features that you can use to jazz up your report.

Glossary

Civil war when two or more groups living in the same country fight each other for control of all or part of the territory.

Climate the average weather of a certain place at different times of the year.

Communists people who want a system of government in which a single political party rules a country with the job of ensuring that wealth is shared equally among all people.

Culture a collection of beliefs, traditions, and styles that belongs to people living in a certain part of the world.

Democracy a country that is ruled by a government chosen by all its people through elections.

Dictator a leader who has complete control over a country and does not have to be elected or re-elected to office regularly. Dictators are often cruel and corrupt.

Economy the system by which a country creates wealth through making and trading products.

Empire territories located in several parts of the world that are controlled by a single nation.

Endangered at risk of dying out.

Exported transported and sold outside the country of origin.

Geographical relating to the study of a country's landscape.

Habitat a part of the environment that is suitable for certain plants and animals.

Imported brought into the country from abroad.

Independent self-governing.

Mainland the main part of a country's territory, especially in areas with a lot of islands.

Medieval relating to the Middle Ages, a period of history from A.D. 500 to 1500.

Minority a small section of a community that has a different culture, roots, or views than the main group of people.

Orthodox something that matches an established and traditional view. The Greek branch of Christianity is described as the Orthodox Church.

Peninsula a region of land that is surrounded by water on three sides and attached to a mainland by a narrow strip of land. The word comes from the Latin for "almost an island."

Republic a country that is headed by an elected president.

Roma an ethnic group found across Europe, and especially common in the southeast areas of the continent; Roma people are often referred to as Gypsies because they were once thought to have come from Egypt, but they are more likely to have their roots in south Asia.

Roman Catholic a Christian who follows the branch of the religion based in Rome, Italy.

Species a type of organism; animals or plants in the same species look similar and can only breed successfully among themselves.

Tsunami a giant wave caused by an undersea earthquake, volcanic eruption, or similar violent event that takes place in water; the forces released send out huge waves that sweep over coastal regions.

Bibliography

DeAngelis, Gina. *Greece.* Mankato, MN: Blue Earth Books, 2004.

Frank, Nicole. *Welcome to Greece.* Milwaukee, WI: Gareth Stevens Publishing, 2000.

Routte, Jane. *Greece.* Westminster, CA: Teacher Created Materials, 2004.

http://www.presidency.gr/en/index.htm (official Web site of the president of Greece)

http://www.gnto.gr/ (general information)

http://news.bbc.co.uk/1/hi/world/europe/country_profiles/1009249.stm (general information)

Further Information

NATIONAL GEOGRAPHIC Articles

Zwingle, Erla. "An Invasion that Greeks Welcome." NATIONAL GEOGRAPHIC (August 2004).

Web sites to explore

More fast facts about Greece, from the CIA (Central Intelligence Agency): https://www.cia.gov/library/publications/the-world-factbook/geos/gr.html

Greece has one of the longest histories of any country. Take a tour of its many different periods: http://www.fhw.gr/chronos/en/

The citizens of Athens often had difficult decisions to make. In the story played out here you can read how they decided to punish the city of Mytilene—and how they realized they'd made a terrible

mistake: http://www.bbc.co.uk/schools/ancientgreece/classics/mytilene/intro.shtml

Find out why people from across Greece came to Delphi hoping to see the future: http://odysseus.culture.gr/h/3/eh351.jsp?obj_id=2507

Take a virtual tour of Athens's Acropolis. http://www.vgreece.com/index.php?category=1110

The International Olympic Committee has a Web site devoted to the ancient games: http://www.olympic.org/uk/games/ancient/index_uk.asp

In ancient Greece, children played *astragaloi*, which means "knucklebones." They played with actual knucklebones of sheep. Players threw the bones across the ground and scored points according to how they fell and knocked over their

opponents' bones. The game is still played with little plastic figures: http://www.magicboxint.com/gogos2008UK/gogos.html

See, hear

There are many ways to get a taste of life in Greece, such as movies and music. Here are two Web sites you can visit to see and hear:

Athens News
Find out what the news is in Greece with this English-language newspaper: http://www.athensnews.gr

Demis Roussos
Greece's most famous recording artist is Demis Roussos: http://www.demisroussos.net/gb/pages/home.htm

You can also watch the movies *Mamma Mia* or *The Sisterhood of the Traveling Pants.*

Index

Credits

Picture Credits

Front Cover – Spine: Jim Hiscott/NGIC; Top: Todd Gipstein/NGIC; Low Far Left: Richard Norwitz/NGIC; Low Left: James L. Stanfield/NGIC; Low Right: Annebicque Bernard/Corbis Sygma; Low Far Right: George F. Mobley/NGIC.

Interior – Corbis: John Pierre Amet: 38; Bettmann: 32, 33 up; Christos Blestos: 56 lo; Charles Bowen/Robert Harding: 53 up; George Christakis/epa: 48 lo; Creasource: 57 lo; Rainer Hackenberg/zefa: 30 up; Hulton Deutsch: 33 lo; Yiorgos Karahalis: 57 up; Danny Lehman: 2 left, 6-7, 13 up ; Orestis Pangiotou: 51 up, 51 lo; Robin Utrecht: 43 lo; Paul Pet/zefa: 21 lo; Carl & Ann Pucell: 31 up; Adam Tall/Robert Harding: 44 up; Onne Van der Wal: 54 lo; Behrakis Yannis/Reuters: 43 up; Getty Images: De Agostini: 3 left, 34-35; NGIC: William Albert, Allard: 52 up; Ira Block: 2 right, 14-15, 40 lo, 53 up; Bruce Dale: 18 lo, 54 up; Gordon Gahan: 26 up, 26 lo; Louis Glanzman: 29 up; Edwin S. Grosvenor: 39 lo, 45 lo; H. M. Herget: 24 right, 42 up; James Hiscott Jr.: 1, 3 right, 5, 46-47; Nadia Hughes: 10 lo, 13 lo; Tom Lovell: 27 lo; Borchi Massimo: 28 up; Michael Melford: 16 lo, 41 up; Richard Norwitz: 2-3, 10 up, 12 left, 19 up, 22-23, 31 lo, 40 up; Joel Sartore: 20 lo; Franc & Jean Shor: 36 lo left; James L. Stanfield: 29 lo, 39 up, 45 up; Paul Sutherland: 21 up; Konrad Wothe: 19 lo.

For more information, please call 1-800-NGS-LINE (647-5463) or write to the following address:

NATIONAL GEOGRAPHIC SOCIETY
1145 17th Street N.W.
Washington, D.C. 20036-4688 U.S.A.

Visit us online at www.nationalgeographic.com/books

ISBN: 978-1-4263-0470-5

Printed in the United States of America

Series design by Jim Hiscott.
The body text is set in Avenir; Knockout.
The display text is set in Matrix Script.

Front Cover—Top: Church,Thíra (Santorini). Low Far Left: Arch of Hadrian, Athens; Low Left: Kittens on a bench, Rhodes; Low Right: Docked boats, Hydra; Low Far Right: Olive seller, Athens.

Page 1—Caryatids, Acropolis, Athens; Icon image on spine, Contents page, and throughout: Ancient theater

Produced through the worldwide resources of the National Geographic Society

John M. Fahey, Jr., *President and Chief Executive Officer*; Gilbert M. Grosvenor, *Chairman of the Board*; Tim T. Kelly, *President, Global Media Group*; John Q. Griffin, *Executive Vice President, President of Publishing*; Nina D. Hoffman, *Executive Vice President, President of Book Publishing Group*; Melina Gerosa Bellows, *Executive Vice President, Children's Publishing*

National Geographic Staff for this Book

Nancy Laties Feresten, *Vice President, Editor-in-Chief of Children's Books*
Bea Jackson, *Director of Design and Illustration*
Jim Hiscott, *Art Director*
Rebecca Baines, *Project Editor*
Lori Renda, *Illustrations Editor*
Grace Hill, *Associate Managing Editor*
Stacy Gold, Nadia Hughes, *Illustrations Research Editors*
R. Gary Colbert, *Production Director*
Lewis R. Bassford, *Production Manager*
Nicole Elliott, *Manufacturing Manager*
Maps, *Mapping Specialists, Ltd.*

Brown Reference Group plc. Staff for this Book

Volume Editor: Tom Jackson
Designer: Dave Allen
Picture Manager: Sophie Mortimer
Maps: Martin Darlison
Artwork: Darren Awuah
Senior Managing Editor: Tim Cooke
Children's Publisher: Anne O'Daly
Editorial Director: Lindsey Lowe

About the Author

JEN GREEN received a doctorate from the University of Sussex, United Kingdom, in 1982. She has worked in publishing for 15 years and is now a full-time author who has written more than 150 books for children on natural history, geography, history, the environment, and other subjects.

About the Consultants

KOSTAS VLASSOPOULOS is a lecturer in Greek history at the University of Nottingham, United Kingdom. His research focuses on Ancient Greek social and political history, and he has recently published a book entitled *Unthinking the Greek Polis: Ancient Greek History beyond Eurocentrism* (2007). Dr. Vlassopoulos was born and educated in Greece and has a strong interest in the influence of the ancient Greek tradition on modern Greece and the Western world.

GREG ANDERSON is an associate professor of History at Ohio State University. He is a specialist in the politics and the culture of Ancient Greece. His book *The Athenian Experiment* (2003) explores the formation of the world's first complex democracy. A native of the United Kingdom, he has visited Greece many times, both for study and for pleasure.

Time Line of
Greek History

B.C.

ca 3000 The Cycladic people develop a significant marble industry with major quarries in Naxos and Paros. Cycladic sculptors use this marble to create abstract figures often found in burial contexts.

ca 2000 The Minoans build palaces at Knossos and Phaistos on Crete. These palaces are centers of government, commerce, and art.

ca 1380 The Mycenaeans develop the palace at Pylos, a large center governed by a king.

ca 1200 Mycenaeans on mainland Greece begin to move to villages in the hills. Greeks speaking a Dorian dialect establish themselves in their place.

776 The tradition of holding the Olympic games every four years begins.

750 Homer, a blind poet, composes the *Iliad* and the *Odyssey*.

593 Solon, ruler of Athens, introduces a liberal law code that provides the foundation for Athenian democracy.

490 Persian forces make their first attempt to conquer Greece, but are defeated by allied Greek forces led by Athens and Sparta.

480 Greek forces led by Athens and Sparta defeat Persian armies in the second Persian War.

477 Some 150 Greek city-states join forces to found the Delian League after the end of the Persian Wars. The alliance aims to protect its members against other military threats.

460 The first Peloponnesian War begins due to a power struggle between Athens and Sparta. The war lasts 15 years before it ends in a truce.

449 The architects Iktinos and Kallikrates begin to build the Parthenon in Athens, the temple of Athena Parthenos.

431 The second Peloponnesian War begins as Athens fights the Peloponnesian League, led by Sparta, for control of Greek areas. After 27 years of fighting, Athens is defeated, with disastrous economic losses.

399 The Athenian philosopher Socrates is found guilt of corrupting youth; he takes poison.

380 The philosopher Plato founds the Academy at Athens.

323 Alexander the Great, king of Macedon, dies after defeating the Persians and expanding Greek influence as far as Egypt, northern India.

146 The Romans attack and defeat Corinth; Greece becomes part of the Roman Empire.

A.D.

267 Goths sack Athens, Corinth, Sparta, and Argos after 10 years of raids on Greek territory.

391 The Roman emperor Theodosius closes pagan temples in Greece, eventually bringing the end of the Olympic games.

395 The Roman Empire splits in two. Greece becomes part of the eastern section, the Byzantine Empire.